mm gillis-gambrell

To my Family—those assigned, and chosen. Thank you for calling out what you saw until I saw it myself. Thank you for holding and blessing all of my broken. Thank you for your support.

Also

To John Mulaney, whose brilliant humor truly kept me alive this long.

And most of all

To Michael, for helping me write poetry that feels like light. I love you more than words.

THE ORDER:

- Eden
- gustavo
- shayla's eclipse
- i can't look mercy in the eye
- for michael
- environmentalist
- heartache the size of texas
- happy birthday
- JP

- visiting home
- why i do this
- reward if found
- wise old wardrobes
- You are Katherine
- temp check
- Silent Anchor
- touch me

For Deborah,
who saw the light
in me long
before I did.

all love ___

- My friend, Elam
- all i know is i was blind
- come with it
- finding soft again
- now i see
- sierra
- For John
- father nose best
- dead beat

- ww1
- george
- in this dream II
- 5 for fighting
- i feel nothing and that's fine
- goodbye CO
- different
- wes
- rough drafts

- screwdrivers
- my suicide note
- i miss cigarettes but i don't miss you
- girl by the water
- III

- in this dream III
- hollow house
- faulted faith: an ode to cs lewis' 'As The Ruin Falls'
- Dylan, I miss the shit out of you
- only the good
- a sinner's sutures

- august tenth twenty eighteen
- in this dream I
- it might be okay

III

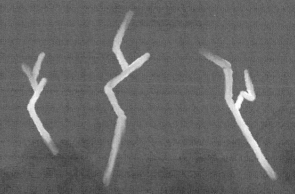

mm gillis-gambrell

Eden

I remember every little thing. The slight shift of your eyes as you thought of your next clever comeback. The way your hand slid up my dress like a snake in a garden. How you said my name like it was a compliment.

I got kicked out of Eden and I didn't even get to keep you.

gustavo

there is a moment, in the past

there is a boy, walking along a railroad track

watching a charm of hummingbirds

drift back and forth across the sky

he wants to write about the way they sway

like a pendulum

like lovers

he wants to dance with them

shayla's eclipse

Something happened to you that day

The moon knocked down the switch for a spell

And real darkness fell over the face of the deep in you

Something about the practicality of it undid you, I think

For three minutes

In the pitch black of day

You finally knew where you were

With all the pounding hearts in town, looking up
into nothing

I bet you kept your sunglasses on, felt understood
by the pounding

By the passing, galactic halo

But in the darkness and in the knowing

Like a dog taken off its leash

Or maybe just like a woman liberated by the space
to be undone

Spirit beaming in the shelter of shadow

gillis-gambrell

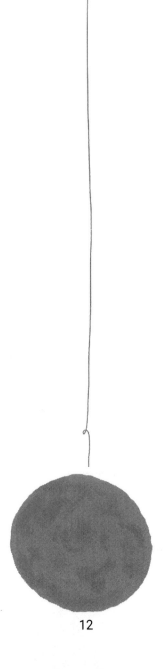

i can't look mercy in the eye

You give me the bread of life

And I fill my mouth with dirt

You give me your cup to drink of

And I drown myself in poison

You give me your shoulder to rest on

And I lay my head upon stone

You offer me your home

And I choose

I choose

To lie in the dirt I eat

You give like you are wounded and running out of time
to give me my inheritance

You give like I am wounded too,
like only your spilled blood will keep my heart beating

You give like you are more concerned with my death
than your own

You give and give and give

And all I have for you are reasons I don't want your gifts

Don't think I need them

Don't think I deserve them

And now I am more afraid than ever

That I have run out of reasons not to take you up
on your offer.

"Where will I put my stone to sleep? And my poison
to die?"

You give me an idea.

I will bury them in the dirt.

I have run out of reasons not to come home.

for michael

These are the thoughts I find myself sleeping next to

In the smallest hours of the morning

I think of all the people

Who had locked themselves away

In the castles I stormed

The ones who hid themselves

Amongst the forests and fog

How I got lost in the woods trying to find them

And by the time the sun is rising

My mind lands on you and your easy disposition

How there were never any smoke and mirrors

Just your gentle eyes

How when you look at me

The sunlight slants into the room

Reaching each corner

Like it's pointing at everything

There were no secret passageways

No traps set amongst the foliage

Just your lover's heart

Pounding like an extravagant holiday parade

And mine next to it

Clapping along to each ecstatic beat

environmentalist

I want to leap across forests

From tree top

To tree top

Like great, green clouds

All bouncing and swaying

As I only dance close enough

And just far enough

From the earth

To still love it

III

heartache the size of Texas

I am the product of an overly emotional control freak
and an under-emotional flight risk

I am the culmination of opposites repelling
and cheating the system

Shattered mugs and bruises

Taught me to trap dreams of joy in glass structures

Kept high up on the furthest shelf

Like snow globes collected by a child

Raised in sweltering heat

I am the child

Dreaming of a still home

Of a heart that does not tremble at the sound
of broken glass

I am the bruise

I am ready to heal

happy birthday

Depression comes over unannounced, even on birthdays. He showers me in kisses and congratulates me. Gives speeches and tells me he looks forward to many more years together. His arms around my waist and his hands around my neck feel exactly the same.

I am eighteen today. I am drowning. I am so, so tired.

JP

I fell in love with your family anecdotes

The eager tones in your voice as you painted
your shimmering, childhood winters

Your youthful delight in picking the perfect Christmas tree

Your memories of golfing and waiting for ice cream
with bubbling anticipation

Your face as you remembered being the sibling
between your parents, as they swung you so far up

Your certainty that nothing was higher than this

Is that why you disappeared? Did you get lost
somewhere, there, in the past?

Even if it isn't to me, I hope you find your way back here.
Your family misses you.

visiting home

Someone tell the tree leaves to stop dancing at me like that.

Can't they see I have to leave?

why i do this

It's when my eyes behold the words

And not a moment sooner

Does my mind exhale.

I go through the day, brain ablaze

Starting forest fires inside of me

Headed in one thousand different directions,

Down one thousand different trails.

But to sprawl out the words before me,

Like an internal map that gets me back to my
peace of minding,

A map to take me down a path, unwinding

Extinguishes those fires.

And somehow, by charting out the flames

The scorching thirst is quenched.

But only for a moment as brief as a breath

As brief as a gust of wind,

That may start the fire up once more.

gillis-gambrell

reward if found

I'm looking for my lover, have you seen him?

He's quite hard to miss.

He is a caution cone orange, sky scraping masterpiece

A kicking and screaming, bleeding heart
with a beat so bomb

He's always dancing

Sometimes his feet just lead him away

He sees over every rooftop and through every
faulty structure

He's quite hard to miss, this brawny, beautiful,
wandering hooligan

You might find him swaggering through your graveyards

Wondering about forever

He found eternity a while back,

But sometimes he goes looking

Check your dirt roads and mountaintops

gillis-gambrell

He prone to soul seeking, there in the silence.

He's quite hard to miss,

With his head in the clouds

His laughter, thundering as his shoulders
catch the raindrops

My silly, solemn, roaming giant.

Sometimes he just needs to explore

Needs to let the rain fall down upon him

So that he might conjure up memories

Of a roof that never leaks

And come rushing back to me.

I'm looking for my lover, have you seen him?

He's quite hard to miss.

But if you find him, tell him there's a girl
waiting for him back home.

Tell him she misses him quite so.

wise old wardrobes

The sidewalks back home assume things about me

The sunset calls me names I no longer go by

But here, past the border of all that I've known

Wise old wardrobes tell me secrets

Young, fresh bookshelves tell me lies

And I am caught in between these trying fixtures

Falling in love

With every breath I take

Everything I see

You are Katherine

Here we are

At our tables

Listening, trying to understand

How Katherine enjoyed the show last Tuesday

Or maybe even discussing policy

Here we are

In line at the shop

Refreshing our timelines and feeds

Looking for an everlasting bit of good news

To transcend this month's freshest brutality and
fiercest bronzer

And again

We are here on our runs—

Racing past the cafes and the complex of that friend
who you've talked to less and less as the years pass by

Trusting our guts that if we push harder

We will outrun whatever brought us to the stretch of
pavement in the first place

The swimsuit or barista who hasn't glanced back

Here we are

Trying to silence our taboo buzzer hearts

Sitting deep inside our chests

Dying for answers

Listening, trying to understand

If we are seen and loved

By those at the table,

Or in front of us in the queue,

Scanning for truth

Up on the balcony of the second story flat,

Behind the bar of the coffee shop,

Searching for nothing more than love, even there,
in the anxious cavities that house every finding
as we traipse along.

temp check

The crowd is overwhelming and I am breaking a sweat

When the others have gone, I am cold

How nice it would be

Not to be tossed by the wind

Nor singed by the sun

What a concept

To feel just right

gillis-gambrell

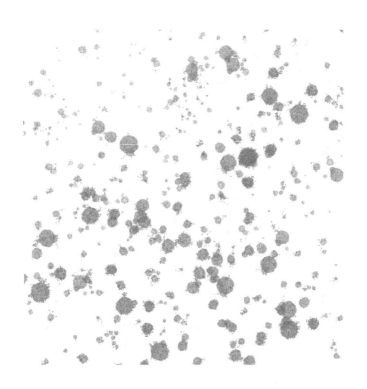

Silent Anchor

Some days I am weak

And nuclear bombs or fireworks—

I can't remember which—

Live within the cage of my lungs

Some days I am drowning

And I do not resist the weight

Sitting at the bottom of the ocean floor

I hold on to this old, rusted anchor

That listens

And sometimes listens harder

So that I become ungrateful and bitter
that it does not speak up

But it is here

And so I lean

With or without sound waves—

gillis-gambrell

I am enveloped in this flow

Pursued by the pressure

Of the heat beneath my feet

Here on the seafloor

And I am here

So I wait

In humble expectation

For the wind to stir the waters

And the waters to stir something else

Something hidden from my eyes

Something inside of me

Waiting to be hauled up

To break through the surface

And set sail

And I do not resist the wait

touch me

I want to feel your hands everywhere

I want to feel them asking God, "How did You know where to start?"

gillis-gambrell

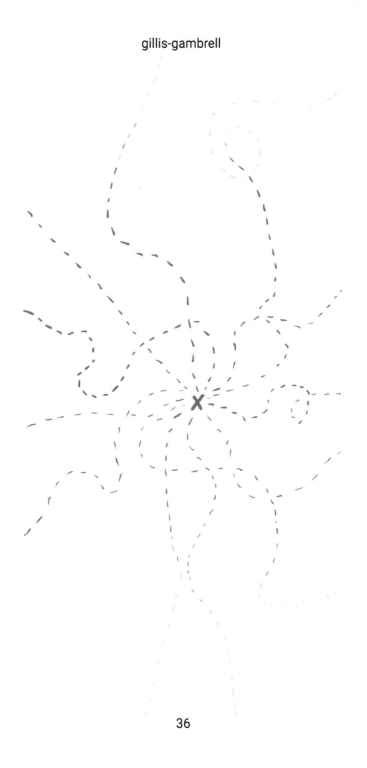

III

My friend, Elam

Full on thoughts

And eye freckles

The universe on backs of paper receipts

Expanding my mind

Explaining ourselves

Explaining The Self

Stopping all time

For profound moments

And awkward laughter

Over first kisses

And natural disasters

Step outside yourself

Cross these boundaries

For the sake of knowing

And think softer

For the sake of sweeter thoughts

Than you have yet to find

all i know is i was blind

Evil fleeing like there's a warrant

All my shame swept into you like a current

All I did was say Your name

And I was saved

I am saved

come with it

come with it

your trembling muscles

and aching lungs

bring your tired eyes

and i'll place a thousand kisses on your face

i'll leave you room to grow

or even room to die

but i will remember

how the freckles on your left shoulder made me
forget my name

it was just an eggshell, love

don't let it break you

or do

and i will remind you

how sweet it all is

gillis-gambrell

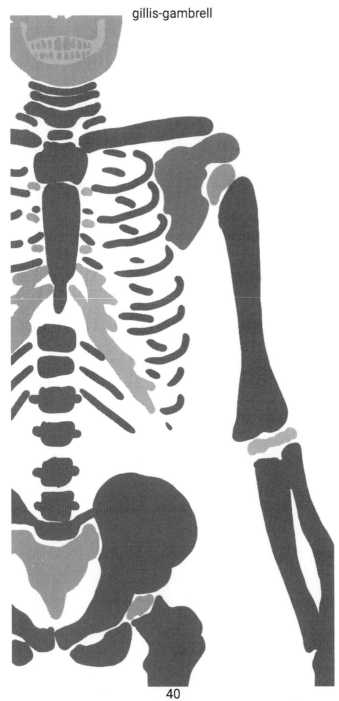

finding soft again

The way he puts his hands on me

Like his fingertips are praying

His palms tell me it's like holding clouds

The callouses built upon the surface of him

Cry

Like I am something soft

That he had once known

The way he keeps his eyes on me

Like he's hungry

Like he's full

Like what else could he possibly ask for?

now i see

Somewhere amidst the breakers and waves

Of the shattered glass and aching chests

Your steadiness found my trembling hands at midnight

When all the places I never thought I'd end up

Became my home

Just a word from you revived this tired heart
that was ready to let go

Laid bare in my own grave

Because I thought to catch my breath

I'd have to breathe my last

Then you showed up and made a way

You made a way

sierra

The miles and time have stretched us thin

Like paper

Like ice

Hearts made of the same

Starting to beat again

And then suddenly

Drums are pounding

And tires spinning

And I'm wondering

Hoping

That there will be no more notes

And time will be all that's frozen

And you'll get to stay where your heart is warm

And the air is thick with love

And it's like we never left for a moment

For John

When the world stops spinning

But our hearts are still breaking

When the questions are answered

But there are still no solutions

When the line goes flat

But we're forced to keep breathing

What do we do

When the wind takes the ashes

But your absence is just as tangible

As your presence

And what do we do

When you and the time both pass

But the pain never passes away

father nose best

I have my father's nose

and his love of all the wrong things

the ocean is his poison

tides that pull him away from me

like the moon holds back water

from the shore

but like that water, that man and I

have known many a tide

and found our way back once more

My mother willed me her mouth

and a mind that won't sit still

it is a sweeping lighthouse

searching for meaning,

for the iceberg,

or on its best days, hope

that the sun will rise and the lost will be found

Dead beat

I was supposed to be fine by now. I was supposed to have accepted your willful absence. Gripped the truth in my hands, bit with grit the reality in my face. But it's like I've been blind this whole time. Groping in the dark for answers, for better odds, for anything that's not the truth. I've spent two years running. That's all I've been doing. Running and running and running, wearing myself out trying to escape facing that awful, ungodly, heart-breaking truth.

You left. You said, "Surely this isn't the place for me any-more," and that was it. You argue that it wasn't so simple, that you wanted to return every day, that it was the hard-est thing you've ever had to do...but I don't know how anything could have been that complicated if you weren't compelled enough to come home.

I saw you today. Your hair is graying. I'm not fine at all.

ww1

What if God had been watching

Would he have laughed

At all of the dots wandering

From one place then back again

From one end of the labyrinth's muck

To the next

And would he have wiped away the Fog and splatter

To continue watching

Somme say he looked away

Or perhaps the Old Man is blind

With no choice but not to see us

Down in brown

And us, no choice

Other than to look up at him or

Our three-sided slop shelter

I read once about a man

Who spat in the dirt

gillis-gambrell

Wiped the dark paste

On a blind man's eyes

And made him see

No coincidence how

That holy mud taught me

That God can't watch

What he doesn't see

Loving dirt or lost, looming deity

Let me not choose God

Let me choose the mud

With that persistence unbroken

The mud that stared right back

And from whose stare we couldn't hide

Let me fall where I lived

Let me lie where I fall

Let me never forget

We all died there

We all died

george

I think of you often

Not in the shadows nor the sunbeams

Not when the bustling crowds are laughing

Appreciatively

The way you would

At the toss of my hair

Or the roll of my eyes

You are not in the fever pitch of midnight

Or even in the warm hands and bright face of devotion

I find you

In the soft of the morning

When it is me

And my untenanted car

The notes of someone else's lost love

And then you

With your fingertips strolling along my
city-street silhouette

Do you remember?

When we decided the light switch-windowed dormitories

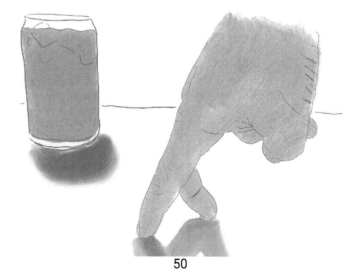

III

Housed the world's brightest electricians?

Do you remember

The way your touch made something inside me

Burn so bright

That I had to run away?

I sense you in the morning

As the sunlight wakes the sleeping city

Something inconsolable and long held back rushes forth

Searching for you on the horizon

in this dream II

In this dream,
You are sitting across from me at a café table.

You have the hem of my sleeve between your index
finger and thumb.

You are saying something that makes me laugh.

"Could we stay like this?"

Somehow I know that we won't,
and that it will be my fault.

You give me a soft smile, and I decide to name
your mouth Mercy.

"We might not be back here for a while, but believe me
you; there will be a café table at the very edge of forever
with your name on it."

There is an ache in my chest, but Your hand in mine is
enough to keep me holding on.

5 for fighting

Tonight I will be sad for you.

Tonight I will weep and gnash my teeth,
resisting my pain

Surrounded by the darkness of my mourning

Tonight I will scream at God

And tell Him you were too young

Because my timing is perfect

And because I know best

Tonight I will be irate with confusion and hopelessness

Tonight I will die with you.

But tomorrow, I will gaze up at the tall evergreens
outside my window

Tomorrow I will breathe in crisp air and blink sleepy eyes
until my morning is in focus

gillis-gambrell

Tomorrow I will force myself out of bed and
become heavy

When thinking of you once I get to the sink
to brush my teeth

Tomorrow I will leave the house for you.

Tomorrow I will sing a bit louder to the songs that
remind me of lighter days

Tomorrow I will walk precisely and listen intently
and laugh recklessly

And do each of these for you

Tonight I will be sad for you.

But tomorrow, I will live for you.

i feel nothing and that's fine

Something here

Between lost and found is

Pleasantly disorienting

I sit at low tide

The horizon is not foggy

Just unfamiliar

The waves crashing the shore

Are all but a memory

But I don't mind

I've come to see that being lost

Isn't such a bad place to find yourself

goodbye CO

My Mountains, you are fading

Though you have stained my eyes

It is time to say goodbye

For new horizons

For empty, unlatched bird cages

For dancing with lions

It is time to say goodbye

Forget me, forget me

I go to stand in sunbeams

That gleam

Through the gaps of gentle snowflakes
like stained glass mosaics

Forget me, forget me

I go to speak with blades of grass

And learn their middle names

Goodbye, My Mountains

I have found a sweeter dream

different

I've done a lot of things to get a guy to like me

Like drive an hour to a soccer game

Or fake pregnancy to get him out of a frat meeting

Or compromise any dignity I thought I had

I've done a lot for the brief glance of an undeserving eye.

I did a backflip off of the Statue of Liberty and stuck the landing on the ground below.

I went back in time and outdrank Hemingway.

I took my helmet off in outer space.

And then you showed up,
and you said you just want to listen,

But all they ever did was take.

And you said you just want to talk,

But the only word they ever said was "more."

And you said you just want to hold hands,

But I'm all white knuckles.

So you listen to my silence, and you speak slowly,
and we go arm in arm.

There's something in the way

Who you are makes space for me to stay me

Something about it is familiar

Like there's always been a secret space for the other

And there are no back flips, no drunken blur,
no space vacuums.

It's just us and some candlelight and the decades, there,
in your eyes.

And it's nice.

wes

If I were to tell you that I have to sleep with the fan off

You would say, "Well, then I have to sleep naked."

If I were to tell you I was afraid of the dark

You would say, "The lights are always on somewhere."

If I were to tell you I was tired of waiting

You would say, "Imagine how Time feels."

If I were to tell you the truth, you'd respect it

Take hold

Bless it, and probably laugh it off

A gentle rough-houser

With wit that leaves me reeling

The way leaves, provoked by the wind,
spin in happy circles

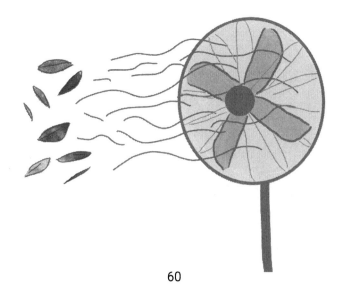

rough drafts

I stand before you

Trembling, tattered

I am wrecked with pencil marks and eraser shavings.

Those who came before you wished me to be well written, complete. They asked for full body paragraphs in clean penmanship. They wanted to be the only ones allowed to see my prose, behold what exquisite words floated around within me. They all left when I tried to expose my disheveled heart. They are all far now.

I watch you see me.

I wonder if you see my eyes saying, "This is all I've got so far." I am tense. I wonder if you will reach for the eraser like the rest did.

Our eyes meet and all you say is, "Masterpiece."
My muscles tighten.

I am suddenly more afraid of being loved than despised.

You don't reach for the pencil either.

I see now, poking out from beneath your collar, your own words, still just scribbles like mine. You roll up your sleeves; the words are scrawled across you like shrapnel, like debris.

You and I are standing in the eye of a hurricane, words spilling from our mouths, etching into our skin as they crash down at our feet.

You watch me see you.

"Masterpiece."

screwdrivers

When I was growing up, my mother drank screwdrivers
and spoke of her childhood

She had two older brothers: one is said to have killed a
man and robbed him

And one robbed my mom

In a way she never wanted to explain

Her younger brother, like a star

So bright but so, so high and dead long before
you know it

Her parents were the kind of people who said things like,
"I turned out just fine."

At night, when I dreamt

I saw my mother

Neck-deep in a cold ocean with a storm overhead

She was alone, unaware of my presence, and she was

Singing

I looked down to find a spool of thread in hand

gillis-gambrell

I spend the rest of the dream frantically trying to lasso
her with the thread

(But to no avail)

Until I wake up

I am grown now

I get hammered some nights and carry memories
of a childhood

That doesn't belong to me

Because I was too busy catching tears

To have my own

When I sleep at night, I stand before a mirror

But when I look across at myself, I am sopping wet

Water spills in through the windows

I cannot sing

These waters do not suit me and I know
I do not swim well

I've run out of orange juice

my suicide note

I couldn't keep living in both worlds

Now, be it heaven or hell

In one, I'll remain

gillis-gambrell

i miss cigarettes but i don't miss you

You take your strangers

And I'll take mine

Becoming one myself

Smoke spilling out of me

Like all these words

I'd never thought I'd scream

How much is enough

When I will never be

There's genocide

And hurricanes

And addiction wreaking havoc on our dreams

So I'm sitting stubbornly

On a curb

Because I can fix any of these

I've been promised a reckoning

A day of victory

Over these things that crash over me

Like breakers

Like unnatural disasters

But it's a forecast that I can't see

So I'll stay on the curb

And let the rain spill onto me

Until the sun comes into view

Setting you and I completely free

girl by the water

We were standing on the split platform of a stairwell

When she told me my bruises were not art

That no one needed to create me any more

That I had already been made

Words that typically echo through my caverns

Found the ocean in me

I had never thought of myself as complete until then

She never loved on accident

She was never spilled

She felt that way sometimes

Knocked over and

On occasions even empty

But she knew the Maker

And she took tear-stained notes as He filled her up

And taught her to purposefully pour once more

gillis-gambrell

She lives by the ocean now and listens to the seashells
tell of their secret sorrow,

No one but she knows the cry of the hollow sea

In them, in me

She has grown kindly familiar to the crashing of waves,
she has never gotten used to letting people cry alone

She is the process by which saltwater heals any wound
willing to wade into it

She is the expectant shore that trusts the incoming tide

She is certainly in most sweet moments of mine

We were standing on the split platform of a stairwell
when I first saw it

Water up to our necks and it hit me

She is refreshing laughter and healing weep

The lament of waves and breakers

She is deep cries out to deep

III

the truth is here

in the constant panic and the settled soul

the cloud nines and the mushroom clouds

in the fever pitch of midnight and the soft swell of noon

we are sustained by great grief

and greater love

we will not do it all so well,

but while we sink, we swim

so if we can learn to laugh

without cutting our losses

that we might stay a while longer

if only for the right of saying so

gillis-gambrell

in this dream III

in this dream, we lie beneath blankets, and you kiss the spot between my shoulder blades

your lips are clouds on my ever-spanning sky

and your eyes are kind, but your hands are tearing at my very seams in all the right ways

we sink into each other like coins drifting to the bottom of a well

and i wish there was nowhere to go

no one to see

no reason to wake up because

in this sweet dream, we never left the bed

hollow house

I own a key to my father's house

That I use when the two-story is empty

To go and see the shining leather couch

To look at the room with the bunk beds

That used to be an office

The room below

That catered to my insomnia and questions

The room across the hall that forgot to hold the escape door open

It is a museum

Of a family I half belong to

Familiar and still

Distant

A reliquary of tokens powerful enough

To undo me on days

When the rain locks me up inside of this house

That never knew me at all

faulted faith: an ode to cs lewis' 'As The Ruin Falls'

I never take my eyes off of myself

Not once have I even glanced at You

Here in my soul's washed up state of cowardice, I find the blinding truth

That I am my own greatest idol

And I never loved you worth a cent

Dylan, I miss the shit out of you

Where did you go

Where were you running so fast

That you forgot to look down

Or look up

Or look back

Or even look ahead of you

And now

Where have you gone

Where

The hell

Have you gone

only the good

My friend...you jackass. You were supposed to clean up your act. You were supposed to be the good looking, old family friend that shows up late to my wedding rehearsal dinner and tells stories of us dancing to "Who Let The Dogs Out" when we were five. You were supposed to dance with me at the reception the next night and whisper in my ear, "You tell me if he hurts you, okay? I know he won't. But you tell me if he ever does. I'll get him good."

You were supposed to kiss my forehead when I had my first baby boy and named him after you. You were supposed to say, "Let's hope he doesn't give you as much hell as we gave our parents." You were supposed to rustle his hair for every holiday you saw him after that.

You were supposed to come over for Fourth of July barbecues. Your son was supposed to teach mine curse words and how to use a slingshot, the way you did with me. You were supposed to laugh at me when my kid said "shit" in front of me for the first time. You were supposed to say, "Sorry, not sorry," once he left the room.

You were supposed to take me out drinking when we were forty and beginning to get worn out by life. You were supposed to look at me sideways from your seat beside me at the bar and bitch me out for getting too uptight. You were supposed to buy my next beer and remind me of when we were five and danced to "Who Let The Dogs Out." You were supposed to say you'd come around more.

You were supposed to be around more.

You were supposed to stick around longer.

You jackass. I needed you here longer.

a sinner's sutures

What would God want to do with someone like me?

His misfit kid who picks at scabs and
never allows Him to rest

As He holds this tension with mercy and discipline

Like a never-ending tug of war

Leaving my wounds open when they need to be aired out

Closing them with more sutures

That we both know I may very well undo

Why would He care

If I bled out or went missing?

His black sheep child who sneaks off into the moonlight

While the masses make it seem like getting lost
was an accident

I crept into the darkness, hoping for some hungry beast
to do its worst

But when I stumbled and injured any image of holy
I might have once had

My Father cut through the night

III

To find my fickle, collapsing heart

And mend it with grace that brought even the shadows to light

Why would He have anything to do with His kin—

Unkind, unfaithful, ungrateful, and blind

To the Love that sees value

In the most pitiful of creatures

His rebellious offspring that forsook all it's heavenly features

For bruises and gashes it believed it deserved?

But still slow to anger, He speaks over me gentle words:

"You can't come for grace that's already with you

You can't run from forgiveness that's already kissed you

Don't resist a love that couldn't resist you

My beautiful, broken beloved

I will mend you each time and again."

august tenth twenty eighteen

When I tell you I love you

It will be in broad daylight

None of this post-midnight

Lapse of judgement

This sleep deprived

Pitch black, slip up

I want it to be purposeful

And I'd rather it be mundane than grandiose

So that I can love you well

When you are doing the dishes

And driving home from work

And asking for some space

And driving me insane

I want to tell you I love you with God
and people as witnesses

So that I may continue to love you
on darker days than that

in this dream I

In this dream

There is a skinny, unending cobblestone path that we stand at the start of.

Sunset casts down the sweetest shadows.

You are here & I am too. There's a certainty in the air that my feet won't grow tired.

it might be ok

Hidden in my heart you'll find

Cries of confusion

And all broken things

It's hard to feel outside your own skin

Hidden in my head you'll find

Marring memories

And such sad stillness

It's hard to think outside your own mind

Hidden in my eyes you'll find

Tears that sting

And lofty dreams

It's hard to see outside your own truth

III

But outside the skin,

Past the mind,

Beyond the line of sight,

Trees sway in breezes

That soften the edges

Of my rigid puzzle pieces

My dreams are mountains

And my laughter is a rushing river

And on this side of heaven

The broken things stay broken

But were beautiful after all

Leave a Review or Connect With the Author

Facebook: mm gillis-gambrell

Instagram: @mmgg.97

Twitter: @mmgg_97

Acknowledgments:

Tess Combs and LeeAnn Siddens: For asking tirelessly when I was going to publish and for never taking "I don't know" for an answer. Also, for taking me in as one of their own.

Nate Combs: For doing the things that allowed this book to actually exist, and for indiscriminately investing in those around you with unparalleled drive and passion.

Shayla Nidever: For bringing my vision of this book's cover into existence, and for all the silent coffee.

Dan and Holly Gillis: For all of their support and provision along the way, of which allowed me to make it this far.

Tammy Thomas: For accepting all of my mess and odd-ness, even without understanding it. And for supporting me in any endeavor, no matter the risk.

Jessi and Xris Johnson: For never having expectations of me and always allowing me to be who I am.

Heather Perry: For seeing the absolute worst of me while believing the best of me.

Evangeline Sonnier: For speaking my language, and never shying away from the ugly. And for never finding it all that ugly to begin with.

Amarachi Chi-Ukpai: For being the embodiment of humor and soul, and for ushering those things into my life since I was five.

Amanda Booth: For hearing the hollow song inside me and singing along.

Elena Evans: For always encouraging me to put my words into the world, and affirming their value.

Elena Evans: She gets two mentions because she deserves it, and I'm trying to make up for the bachelorette incident.

Wesley Russell: For all of the laughter and dark comfort that our friendship brings.

Gustavo Jacobo: For making the world feel better, and for helping me believe in myself and in my abilities. This has carried me through.

Elam Blackwell and his family: For their absurdly generous investment in my endeavors and personhood, and for letting me ask a million questions when their conversations go out of my depth.

Sierra Braukmann: For being so odd and so full of love.

Jacob Sorsoleil and his family: For being full of authenticity and friendship at all times. May John be honored through these words, and may they bring comfort.

Andrew Touma: For giving me Kurt Vonnegut and teaching me to question the answers.

III

Alicia Stevenson and Tracey Wilkinson: For calling out my potential, and for being unbelievably invested teachers.

George: For not hating me after all my hypocrisy and crying, and for being such a bitter-sweet muse all these years. iii

Dylan Cooper and his parents, Billy and Dena: For giving me my first love and first best friend. He is irreplaceable to my heart and I miss him every day.

Karlie Fish: For being an honest-to-God friend. Rough Drafts will always be about her.

Sarah Emano: For Mexico, and for being a truth-bringer.

Michael Gatlin: For showing me C.S. Lewis' work, for Van Morrison, and for being my friend.

76108627R00052

Made in the USA
Columbia, SC
25 September 2019